PREHISTORIC PEOPLE

Troll Associates

PREHISTORIC PEOPLE

by Laurence Santrey

Illustrated by Dick Smolinski

Troll Associates

Library of Congress Cataloging in Publication Data

Santrey, Laurence.
Prehistoric people.

Summary: Discusses the day-to-day life of prehistoric peoples and how they assured their survival by developing tools and refining their hunting techniques.
1. Man, Prehistoric—Juvenile literature. [1. Man, Prehistoric] I. Smolinski, Dick, ill. II. Title.
GN744.S26 1985 573.3 84-8464
ISBN 0-8167-0242-X (lib. bdg.)
ISBN 0-8167-0243-8 (pbk.)

Printed in the United States of America

10 9 8 7 6 5 4 3 2 1

Human beings everywhere have the same basic needs: food, protection from the weather, and safety from dangers. Only after people meet these needs do they have time to play games, to make music or create works of art, or enjoy life in other ways. This is true today, and it has always been true.

In the modern world, most people don't have to spend every minute of their lives meeting their basic needs. We take food, clothing, and shelter for granted. But in the distant past, nothing could be taken for granted. The struggle for survival dominated the existence of prehistoric people.

Prehistoric people are those who lived on Earth before writing had been invented. They did not pass on any written record of their lives from generation to generation. But they did leave clues. These clues give us some information about the way they lived, what they ate, and what they looked like—thousands and thousands of years ago.

The clues left by prehistoric people are bones, teeth, tools, footprints, seeds and nuts, the remains of campfires, and other signs of long-ago life. By studying these clues and where they are found, scientists are able to tell us many things about these ancient people.

Long before people appeared on the Earth, there were many other kinds of animals. Some of these animals, called primates, were apelike creatures that lived in trees. Then, at some time—anywhere from five to fourteen million years ago—some of these primates began to live on the ground and walk on their two hind legs at least some of the time.

We know about these ancient primates because of fossils. Fossils are the remains of animals or plants that have been preserved over the years. Fossil remains also show us that humanlike creatures lived on the grassy plains of Africa about two and a half to three million years ago. These beings were four to four and a half feet tall. They walked upright on two legs all the time. This left their arms and hands free to do many things.

Scientists think that these creatures had low, sloping foreheads with a bony ridge over the eyes, and almost no chin. These ancestors of human beings had faces and hairy bodies like apes. They probably could not talk and did not know how to make tools. And they ate raw plants, birds' eggs, and animals they killed with branches or stones.

During the Stone Age, prehistoric people learned to use their hands to make useful objects we call tools. The oldest tools found by scientists are stone choppers that were probably made about two million years ago. A chopper was a rock that was roughly sharpened on one side. It could be used to dig or cut, scrape or pound.

As more time passed, tools made by prehistoric people became less primitive. One of these tools was a sharp-edged hand axe that was shaped like a pointed leaf. The hand axe could be used for cutting meat, opening clam shells, digging roots from the ground, cracking nuts, or stripping the hide off an animal.

Another kind of stone tool, called a hollow scraper, had a sharp groove on one side. Prehistoric people used the hollow scraper to sharpen a stick into a spear. The development of these tools tells scientists something important about the people who made them. It says that they were more advanced than the people who made only rough choppers.

One of the significant differences between human beings and all other animals is that people have invented tools to make survival and everyday life easier. For example, the spear-stick was a better hunting tool than branches and rocks. And the people who

created it were far more like today's humans than their primitive ancestors were.

From all the tools and other evidence they have found, scientists are able to learn quite a lot about how prehistoric people lived in the Stone Age.

Imagine that you are living more than 500,000 years ago. You're in Europe on what is now the southern coast of France, near the Mediterranean Sea. But you do not have a permanent home. Instead, you travel from place to place with your family and a few other families.

The group that includes your family might be called a tribe—except that there is no word like that in your language. In fact, there are very few words spoken by your people. Language, which is a way of exchanging ideas, is just beginning to develop. The humanlike creatures who lived before your people could not speak at all. Like the other animals on Earth, all they could do was howl and growl and grunt and make other primitive sounds.

It is a spring day. Your people are camped near a river that flows to the nearby sea. Every year they travel here to hunt the elephants, rhinoceroses, deer, and wild boars that come to drink at the river. The best hunters in your group will kill as many of these animals as they can.

The hunters will frighten the animals—perhaps with fire—driving them into an area where they can be trapped. Here the hunters will kill them with sharpened sticks, rocks, and bolas.

A bola is a hunting tool made of three stones wrapped in pieces of animal skin and tied together with leather strips. A hunter twirls the bola over his head, then hurls it at the legs of a running animal. The strips of leather wrap around the legs, and the animal trips and falls. Then the hunters pounce on it.

Back at the camp, some of your people are building a large hut. It is made of tree branches stuck into the sand and lashed together at the top. The hut looks like a very large tent. While the hut is being finished, you and some of the other children gather flat stones and dry twigs and branches. These are needed for the campfire.

When all the stones and branches are in place in the hut, the fire-carrier starts the cooking fire in the center of the stones. The fire-carrier has a very important job. It is up to that person to take burning embers from the last campfire and keep them alive in a stone bowl. If the fire goes out, your people will not be able to cook. They do not know how to make fire and must wait until they come upon a forest fire.

Today, the hunters bring back much fresh meat. And there is other food to go with it. There are nuts and berries and roots from the forest. And there are fish and shellfish from the nearby sea. All day your people gather food. Then, as the sun sets, they go into the hut.

Here, next to the cooking fire, it is warm and safe. The wild animals will not come too close to the hut, for they fear the fire. The meat roasting on the open fire smells good. One of the adults cuts off a large chunk for you, using a sharp hand axe made from stone.

When the meal is done, some of your people wrap themselves in animal skins and go to sleep. Others tell stories, using a few words and hand signs, about the day's hunting and fishing.

You watch a tool-maker knocking chips off a small rock. When the work is done, the rock will be a hand axe. You watch the fire for a while, and then you drift off to sleep.

Prehistoric people continued to change as time passed. They invented more and better tools. They invented stone borers, to make holes in animal hides. They made needles from bones, to sew the hides together for clothing. They made spearheads from antler points and tied them to long sticks. With these weapons they harpooned fish and hunted land animals.

In the ice ages that swept the world less than 100,000 years ago, these hunting and tool-making skills were the key to survival. Creatures that could not adapt to the new,

harsh conditions died out. The survivors, whom scientists now refer to as Cro-Magnon people, adapted well to the cold weather. They moved into caves or built warm, hide-covered dwellings.

Cro-Magnon people showed great intelligence. They made good use of the materials that surrounded them. They also left a kind of written history of their lives. This history is not in words, but in paintings, carvings, and engravings.

These paintings are of animals and hunting scenes, and they are located in caves in France and Spain. They were done in colors made from ground-up rock—more than 30,000 years ago. They show us what woolly mammoths looked like. The hunting scenes show herds of horses and deer, and some animals being hunted and killed with spears.

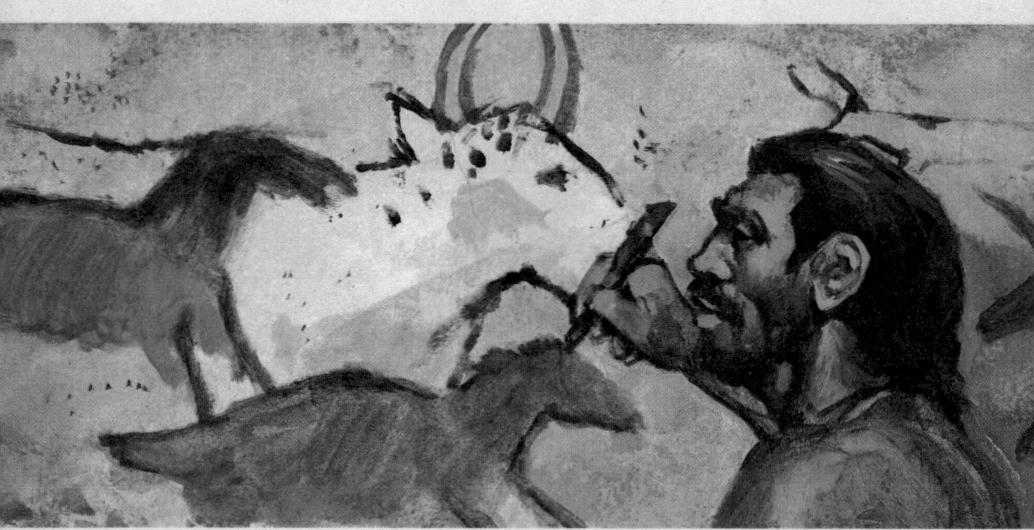

Later paintings also show human beings using bows and arrows. These prehistoric people also decorated their clothing with beads, wore necklaces made of stones and shells, and carved beautiful statues from ivory and from animal bones.

When the glaciers melted and the Earth's climate warmed again, people learned to tame animals, such as sheep, goats, cattle, and pigs. Now the people had a steady food supply without having to hunt it. Some of these people also learned to plant seeds and grow food.

Keeping animals and growing crops made it possible for people to stop wandering from place to place. They settled down and built sturdy, permanent homes. And they formed small communities. Civilization had begun.

Once people settled in one place and had a steady food supply, they had time to invent new things. Some of these early inventions were: baked-clay bowls and storage jugs, used to hold food and water; the wheel; and written language. With the creation of written language, prehistoric times came to a close. That was just 5,000 years ago—a mere tick of the clock of time.